If you were a

Suffix

by Marcie Aboff

illustrated by Sara Gray

PICTURE WINDOW BOOKS
Minneapolis, Minnesota

suffix a letter or group of letters added to the end of a word to change its meaning

Editor: Christianne Jones
Designer: Hilary Wacholz
Page Production: Melissa Kes
Art Director: Nathan Gassman
The illustrations in this book were created with acrylics.

Picture Window Books
1710 Roe Crest Drive
North Mankato, MN 56003
www.capstonepub.com

Looking for suffixes?

Watch for the

Library of Congress Cataloging-in-Publication Data
Aboff, Marcie.
If you were a suffix / by Marcie Aboff ; illustrated by
Sara Gray.
p. cm. — (Word fun.)
Includes index.
ISBN 978-1-4048-4774-3 (library binding)
ISBN 978-1-4048-4778-1 (paperback)
1. English language—Suffixes and prefixes—Juvenile literature.
I. Gray, Sara, ill. II. Title.
PE1175.A24 2008
428.1—dc22
2008006417

Printed in the United States   5619

If you were a suffix ...

Look for the suffixes in **underlined letters** **throughout the book.**

Special thanks to our advisers for their expertise:

Rosemary G. Palmer, Ph.D., Department of Literacy
College of Education, Boise State University

Terry Flaherty, Ph.D., Professor of English
Minnesota State University, Mankato

3

... you would come last!

If you were a suffix, you would be a letter or a group of letters added to the end of a word. By adding a suffix, the meaning of the word changes.

The hope<u>less</u> hippo became hope<u>ful</u> after he won the lottery.

The care<u>less</u> cat became a care<u>ful</u> cat after he used up his eighth life.

$$\$1.00 \\ +\ .25 \\ \overline{\ \ \ \ \ } \\ \$1.25$$

If you were the suffix "er," you would be the one who does something.

The teach**er** taught the bank**er** how to count.

Then the bank**er** taught the bak**er**,

the bak<u>er</u> taught
the farm<u>er</u>,

and the
farm<u>er</u>
taught the
train<u>er</u>.

If you were the suffix "s" or "es," you would make things plural.

The bear and fox ran toward the bush.

Other bear<u>s</u> and fox<u>es</u> hid behind the bush<u>es</u>.

10

One horse jumped over a fence.
Three horses jumped over many fences.

If you were the suffix "ful," you would mean "full of."

The clumsy waiter spilled a **cup_ful_** of coffee all over the king.

To make matters worse, it happened in front of a roomful of people.

If you were the suffix "less," you would mean "without."

The fear<u>less</u> eagle soared
into the end<u>less</u> sky.

The careless elephant almost stepped on the harmless mouse.

The tasteless zebra thought the pretty dress was useless.

If you were the suffix "est," you would state the size of something. You would always be the extreme.

The tallest giraffe and the shortest monkey were best friends.

The **big<u>gest</u>** rhino and the small<u>est</u> bird
were best friends, too.

The four
friends
crossed
over the
wid<u>est</u> river.

17

If you were the suffix "d" or "ed," you would change a word from present tense to past tense.

The frog likes to hop and jump.
The frog hop**ped** on the stones
and jump**ed** into the water.

Mama pig can oink loudly.
She oink<u>ed</u> at the piglets until
they return<u>ed</u> to the pigpen.

If you were a suffix, you could change the spelling of the root word.

The dogs sat by the pool.
They liked <u>sitting</u> by the pool.

If you were a suffix, you might drop a letter and add a new letter. The letter "y" is often replaced by the letter "i."

There were plenty of poppies in the field. The poppies were plent**iful**.

Peacocks have feathers of great beauty. Their feathers are beaut**iful**.

You would be the perfect ending ...

THE END

... if you were a suffix.

FUN WITH SUFFIXES

Cut out 20 pieces of paper and mix them up. On each piece of paper, write one of the suffixes or root words from below. Mix them up. Then, see if you can match them and put the words back together. Next, make your own list and have a friend match the words. You can even time each other and see who can match the words the fastest.

brave ly
move ment
dark   ness
interest ing
lemon   ade

neighbor hood
wood en
free dom
taste ful
use less

Glossary

past tense—a verb showing something that happened in the past

plural—more than one

present tense—a verb showing something happening in the present moment

root—the basic meaning of the word

suffix—a letter or group of letters added to the end of a word to change its meaning

To Learn More

More Books to Read

Draze, Dianne. *Red Hot Root Words.* Austin, Tex.: Dandy Lion Publications, 2003.

Heinrichs, Ann. *Prefixes and Suffixes.* Chanhassen, Minn.: Child's World, 2006.

LoGiudice, Carolyn, and Kate LaQuay. *Spotlight on Vocabulary, Prefixes and Suffixes.* East Moline, Ill.: LinguiSystems, Inc., 2005.

On the Web

FactHound offers a safe, fun way to find Web sites related to topics in this book. All of the sites on FactHound have been researched by our staff.

1. Visit www.facthound.com
2. Type in this special code: 140484774X
3. Click on the FETCH IT button.

Your trusty FactHound will fetch the best sites for you!

Index

Look for all of the books in the Word Fun series:

If You Were a Compound Word
If You Were a Conjunction
If You Were a Contraction
If You Were a Homonym or a Homophone
If You Were a Noun
If You Were a Palindrome
If You Were a Prefix
If You Were a Preposition
If You Were a Pronoun
If You Were a Suffix
If You Were a Synonym
If You Were a Verb
If You Were Alliteration
If You Were an Adjective
If You Were an Adverb
If You Were an Antonym
If You Were an Interjection
If You Were Onomatopoeia